WHY the EARTH QUAKES

WHY

the EARTH QUAKES

JULIAN MAY

Illustrated by LEONARD EVERETT FISHER

Holiday House · New York

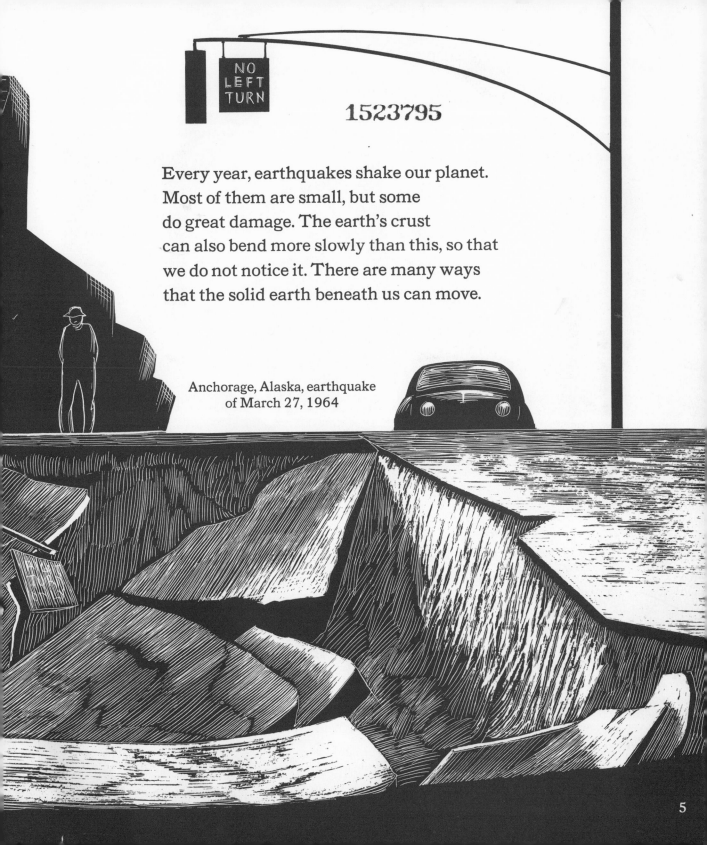

1523795

Every year, earthquakes shake our planet.
Most of them are small, but some
do great damage. The earth's crust
can also bend more slowly than this, so that
we do not notice it. There are many ways
that the solid earth beneath us can move.

Anchorage, Alaska, earthquake
of March 27, 1964

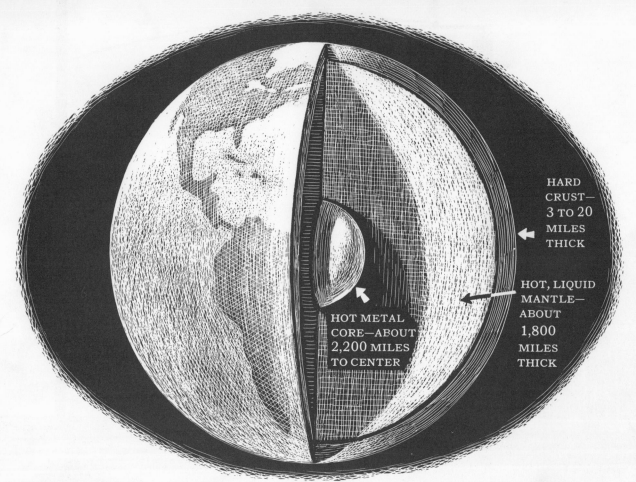

HARD CRUST— 3 TO 20 MILES THICK

HOT, LIQUID MANTLE— ABOUT 1,800 MILES THICK

HOT METAL CORE—ABOUT 2,200 MILES TO CENTER

What is inside the earth

Our world is hard only on the outside.
Its crust is made of solid rock.
Below this is the mantle, a layer of hot,
thick, liquid rock. The earth has
a center made of metal that is even hotter
than the mantle.

In some places on earth, volcanoes
pour out melted rock, called lava.
It flows like thick batter
and gets hard as it cools.
Lava might be made of melted rock
from the underpart of the earth's crust,
down near the hot mantle. Perhaps some lava
even comes from the mantle itself.

Active volcano,
Hawaii

CRUST

LAVA
LAKE

MANTLE

Old Faithful geyser, Yellowstone National
Park, Wyoming, caused by ground water
that is heated by hot rocks deep underground

Many scientists believe that the rock
of the mantle is able to flow,
something like lava. This flowing
may cause not only earthquakes and volcanoes,
but also geysers and hot springs.
It may even set the shape of the earth's continents.

Here is one way that the mantle might flow.
When cold liquid mixes with warmer liquid,
flowing movements called convection currents
are formed. The picture shows
convection currents in a pan of water
heating on a burner.

You can see convection currents.
Get a glass of ginger ale with ice cubes.
Hold it to the light and look
at the liquid close to the ice.
You will see flowing, swirling movements.
Liquid cooled by the ice is mixing
with warmer liquid from the rest
of the glass.

If there are convection currents
in the mantle, they must move very slowly.
Liquid rock is heavy.
And it is also pressed down tightly
by the heavy crust above it.
The part of the mantle nearest
the hot core of the earth
is squeezed so tightly that it probably
cannot flow at all.

Arrows show flowing
convection currents

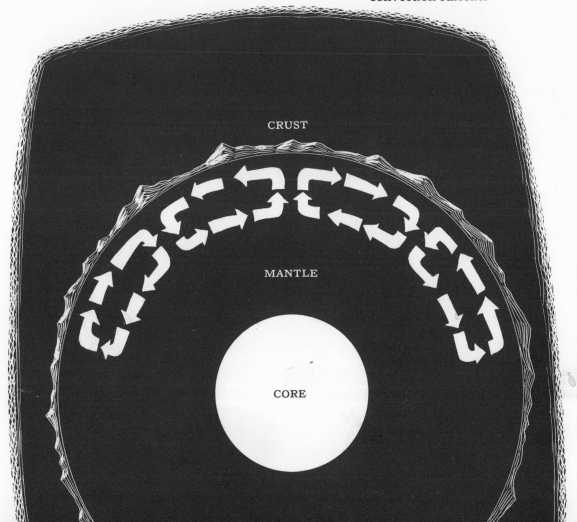

CRUST

MANTLE

CORE

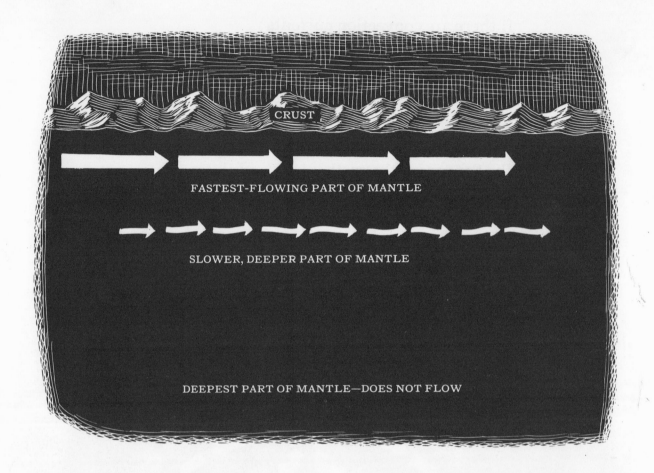

CRUST

FASTEST-FLOWING PART OF MANTLE

SLOWER, DEEPER PART OF MANTLE

DEEPEST PART OF MANTLE—DOES NOT FLOW

Some scientists think that the part
of the mantle that flows
is not very far below the crust.
The convection current in the mantle
might move somewhat the way
this picture shows. The mantle
probably moves less than an inch a year.

Hotter parts of the mantle from deeper
inside the earth move upward.
This happens because hot liquid
is not as heavy as cooler liquid.
In some places where the mantle currents
move upward, the earth's crust may break
and spread apart.

Hot rock acts like hot water

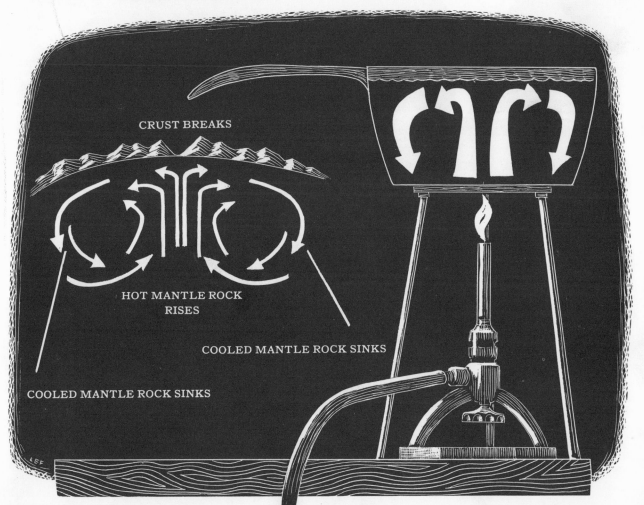

CRUST BREAKS

HOT MANTLE ROCK
RISES

COOLED MANTLE ROCK SINKS

COOLED MANTLE ROCK SINKS

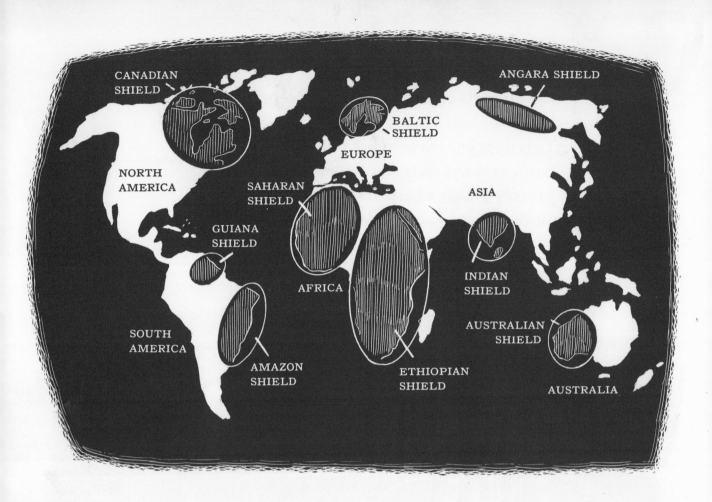

Perhaps this is what caused some kinds
of very old rocks to form.
The oldest rocks known on earth were once
red-hot and liquid. They oozed up
and hardened and became the first
continents, or dry masses of land.
These old "shields," as they are called,
are more than two billion years old.

The continental shields are made of granite.
Younger granite rocks lie under the other
parts of the continents.
These rocks did not come from volcanoes,
but rather were pushed up very slowly
by the flowing mantle beneath.

A continent

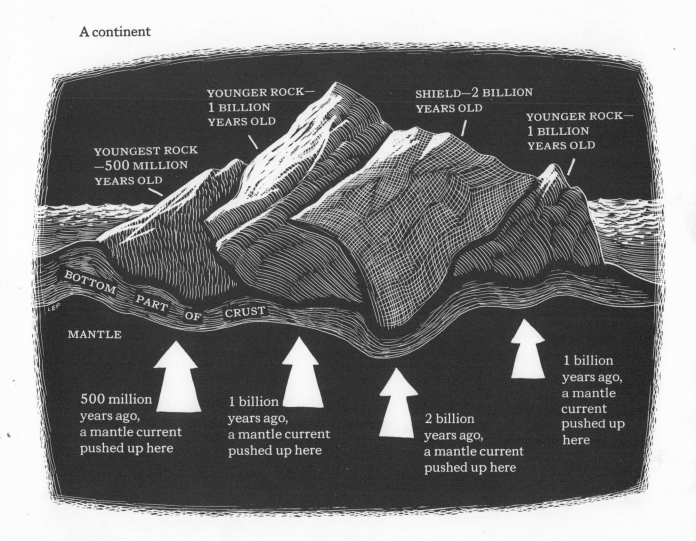

YOUNGER ROCK—
1 BILLION
YEARS OLD

SHIELD—2 BILLION
YEARS OLD

YOUNGER ROCK—
1 BILLION
YEARS OLD

YOUNGEST ROCK
—500 MILLION
YEARS OLD

BOTTOM PART OF CRUST

MANTLE

500 million
years ago,
a mantle current
pushed up here

1 billion
years ago,
a mantle current
pushed up here

2 billion
years ago,
a mantle current
pushed up here

1 billion
years ago,
a mantle
current
pushed up
here

15

Convection currents in the mantle
seem to be at work right now. They may
cause underwater mountain chains
called ocean ridges. The huge
Mid-Atlantic Ridge goes all the way
from Antarctica nearly to the North Pole.

The Indian Ocean and South Pacific Ocean
have ridges too. The picture shows
how they may be formed.

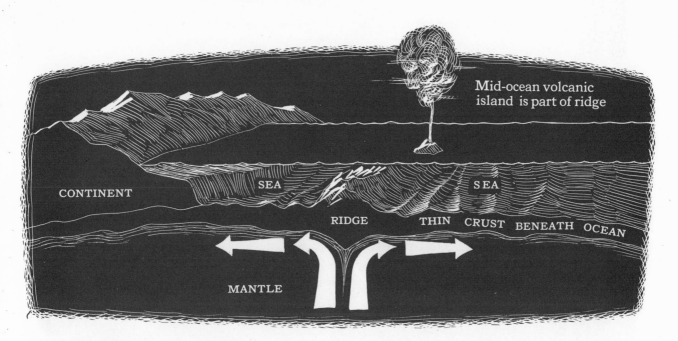

Mid-ocean volcanic
island is part of ridge

CONTINENT

SEA

SEA

RIDGE   THIN   CRUST   BENEATH   OCEAN

MANTLE

Ocean ridges of the world

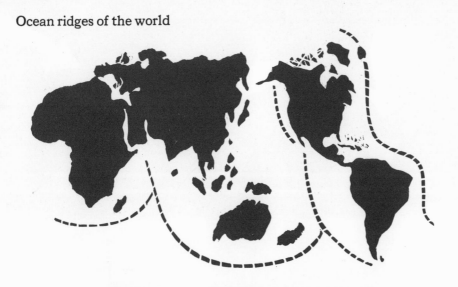

Convection currents in the crust
seem to flow *downward* as well as upward.
This happens when mantle rock gets cooler,
which makes it sink. Some parts
of the ocean floor have deep valleys
called trenches. They may be
places where the crust is sinking.

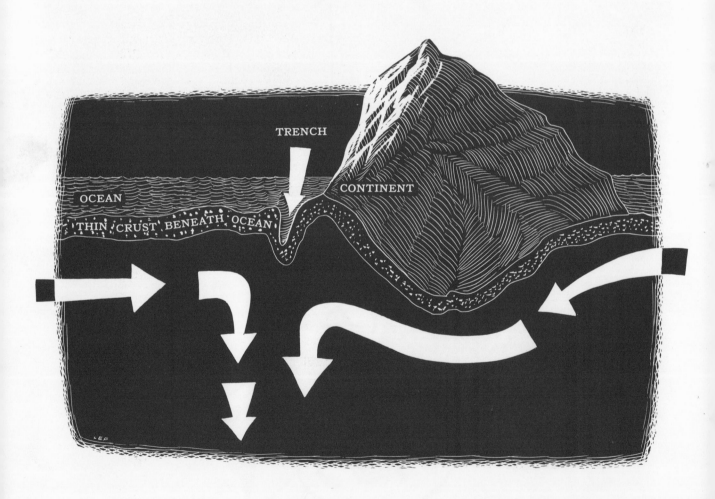

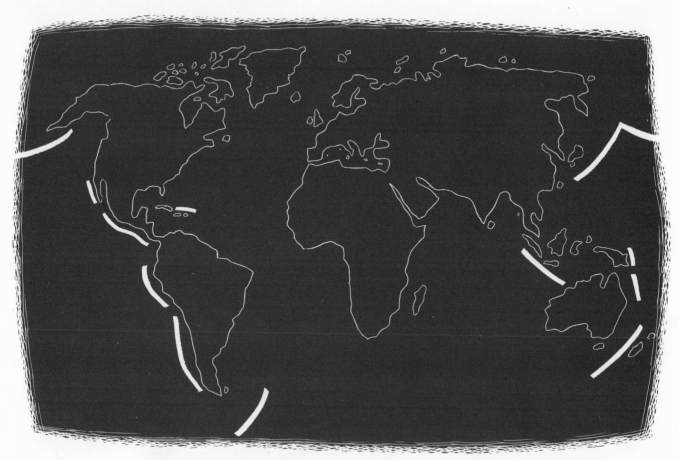

Ocean trenches of the world

Trenches usually are near
the edges of continents, or else
near island chains.
The trenches of the Pacific make
a great ring, with a branch
going into the East Indies.

Convection currents go up and down—
and they may also move from side to side.
This could explain why
some parts of the earth's crust
have huge cracks, called faults.
One of these faults goes through California.

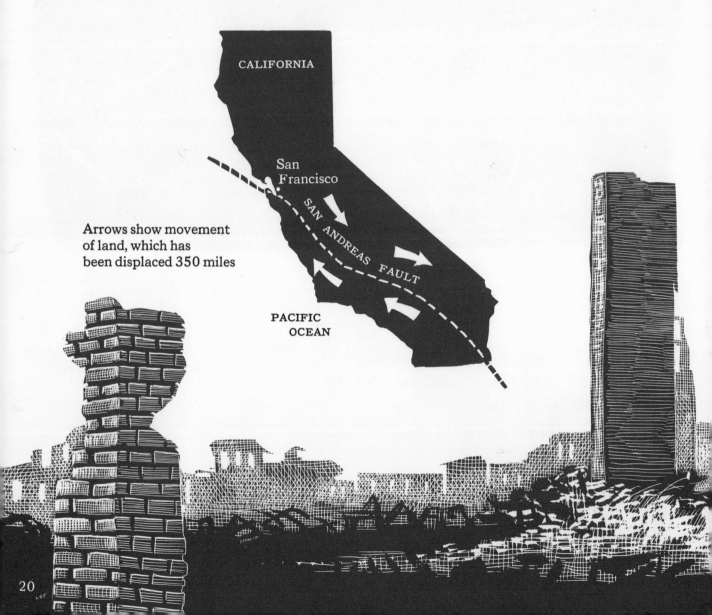

CALIFORNIA

San
Francisco

SAN ANDREAS FAULT

Arrows show movement
of land, which has
been displaced 350 miles

PACIFIC
OCEAN

Faults are interesting, because
they are often places that have earthquakes.
A quake is a sudden movement
of the earth's crust. It is different
from the slow movements
that build mountains and trenches.
The San Andreas Fault in California
has had many small earthquakes
and some large ones.

Great San Francisco
earthquake, 1906

Scientists think that the
slow-flowing mantle pulls and pushes
at the hard crust. For a long time
the crust does not move.
But then it suddenly breaks
at the weakest place, the fault.

The fault blocks may move upward, or downward, or slip to the sides. Sometimes there are several different movements all at once. Strong earthquakes may cause terrible damage if they move the land under people's houses.

UP-AND-DOWN MOVEMENT

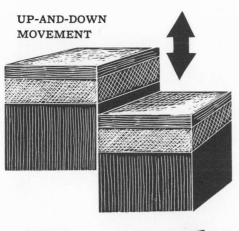

SIDEWAYS MOVEMENT

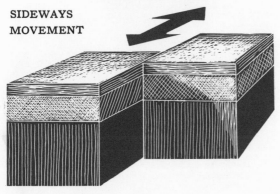

These are the parts of the world
that have the most earthquakes.
Look again at the maps on pages 17 and 19.
How do they help prove
that rising and sinking movements
of the earth's crust
are a cause of earthquakes?

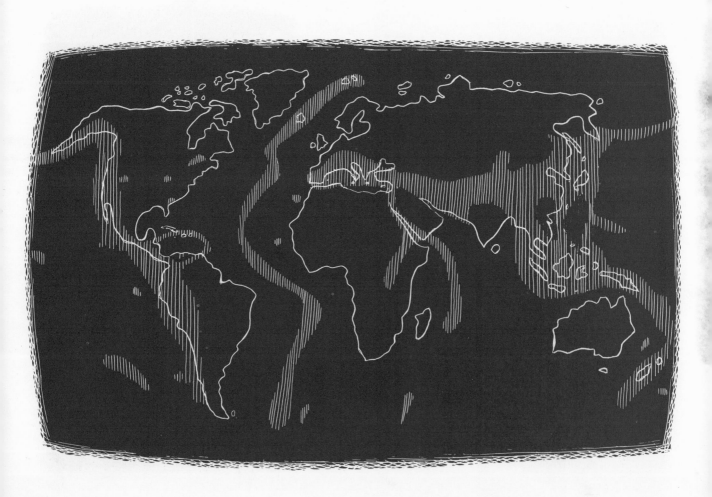

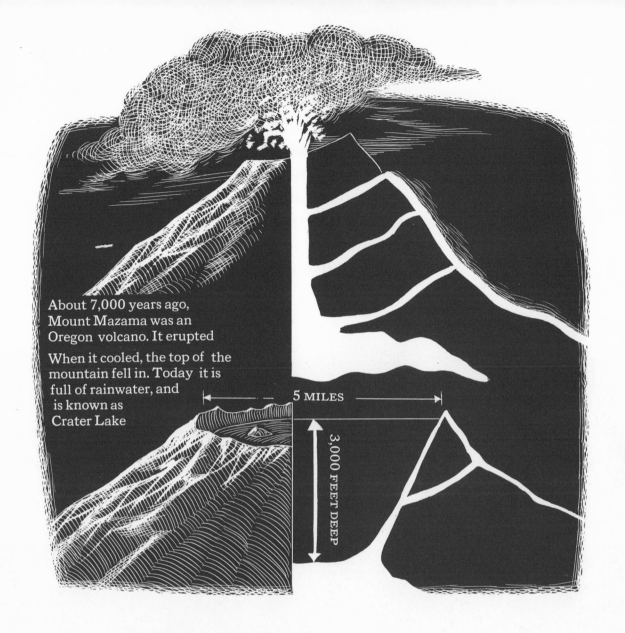

About 7,000 years ago,
Mount Mazama was an
Oregon volcano. It erupted

When it cooled, the top of the
mountain fell in. Today it is
full of rainwater, and
is known as
Crater Lake

5 MILES

3,000 FEET DEEP

Volcanoes are weak places
in the crust where liquid rock is able
to flow out. They do not act alike.
Some explode and destroy everything
around them. Others flow quietly.

Volcanoes are probably caused
by several different kinds of mantle
movements. The picture shows places
on earth that have many volcanoes.
Look at it, and look also
at the pictures on pages 17, 19, and 24.
Think about what you see.

Volcanic regions of the world

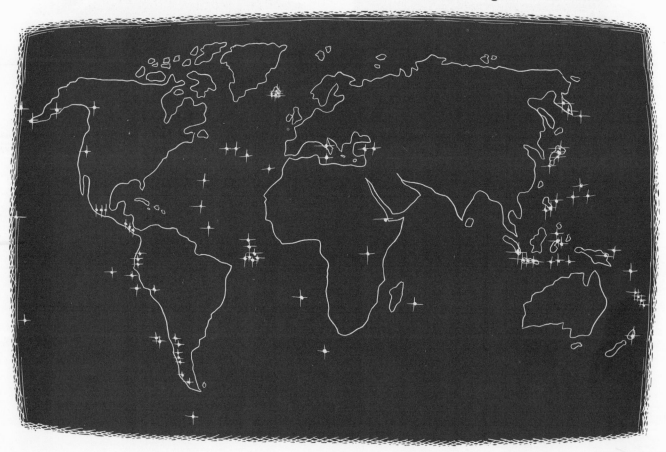

Mayon volcano in the Philippines erupts often

The part of the earth around
the Pacific Ocean that has the most
volcanoes and earthquakes is called
the "ring of fire." It seems to be a place
where the earth's crust is sinking slowly—
and setting off a lot of fireworks as it goes.

There are volcanoes and earthquakes
along the ocean ridges too.
But many of these volcanoes erupt below water,
and don't make much fuss. The underwater
earthquakes are usually noticed only by
scientists who watch earthquake-detecting
instruments called seismographs.

Very strong underwater earthquakes or
eruptions may cause giant waves.
These are called tsunamis, a word taken from
the Japanese. Japan has suffered
from these waves, and so have the islands
of the East Indies, where both
ridges and trenches are common.

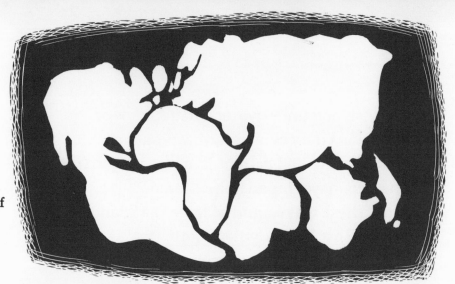

The world of
150 million
years ago

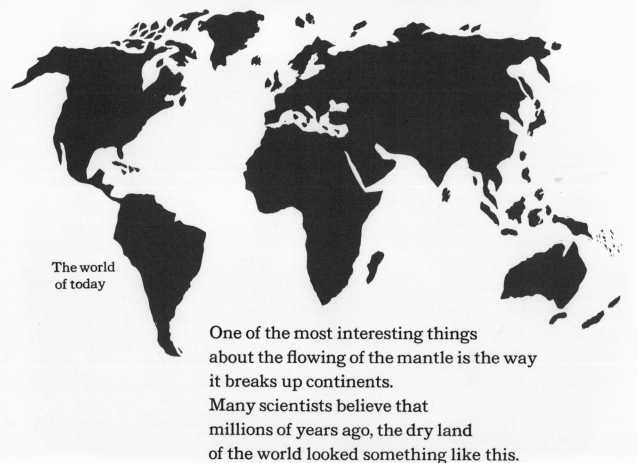

The world
of today

One of the most interesting things
about the flowing of the mantle is the way
it breaks up continents.
Many scientists believe that
millions of years ago, the dry land
of the world looked something like this.

This great "supercontinent" was made
of granite, just as today's continents are.
The granite of the continents
is not as heavy as the rock of the ocean floor.
And so the supercontinent "floated"
on the heavier rock beneath it.

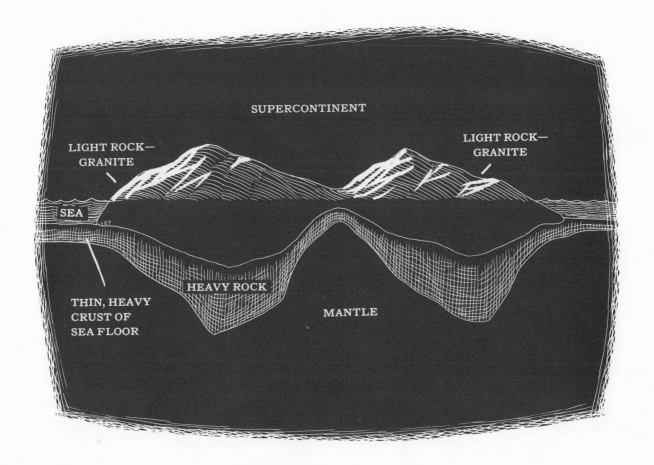

Convection currents in the mantle beneath
pushed at faults in the supercontinent.
The granite slowly broke apart.
Hot mantle rock welled upward
into the crack, cooled, and became hard.
But new, liquid rock kept coming up.
The continents were pushed farther and farther
apart in this way.

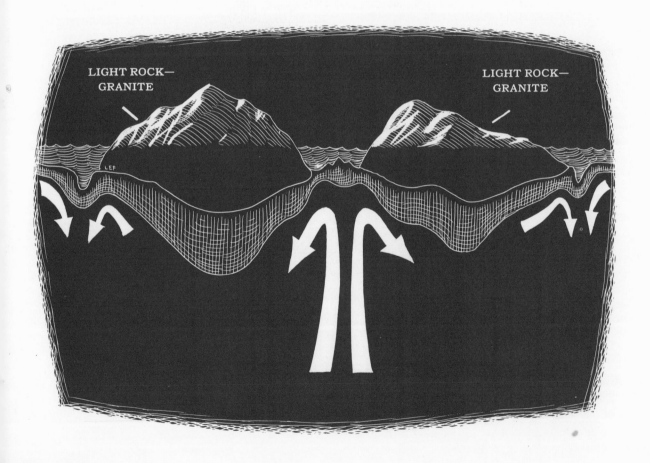

LIGHT ROCK—
GRANITE

LIGHT ROCK—
GRANITE

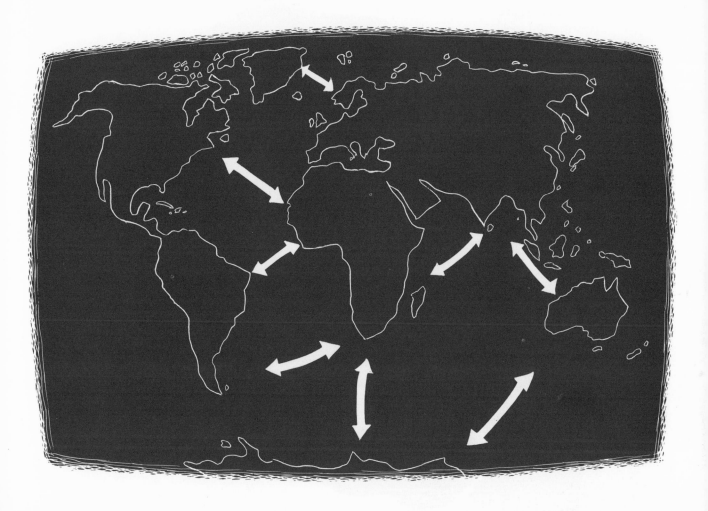

The Mid-Ocean ridges have cracks
down their centers today. Probably the mantle
is still slowly welling up, slowly pushing
North and South America farther away
from Europe and Africa. And in the
Indian Ocean, Australia is moving away
from India and Antarctica.

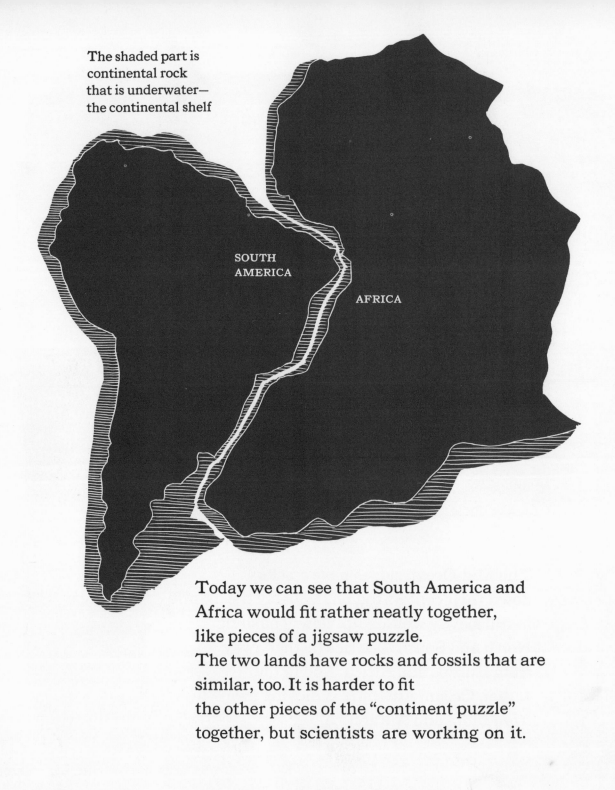

The shaded part is
continental rock
that is underwater—
the continental shelf

SOUTH
AMERICA

AFRICA

Today we can see that South America and
Africa would fit rather neatly together,
like pieces of a jigsaw puzzle.
The two lands have rocks and fossils that are
similar, too. It is harder to fit
the other pieces of the "continent puzzle"
together, but scientists are working on it.

The parts of the continents near
the sinking mantle behave differently.
The continental granite is light.
It does not sink down deeply into a trench as the
nearby ocean-floor rock does.
Instead, the continent rock wrinkles
and piles up. It forms mountains
near the trenches.

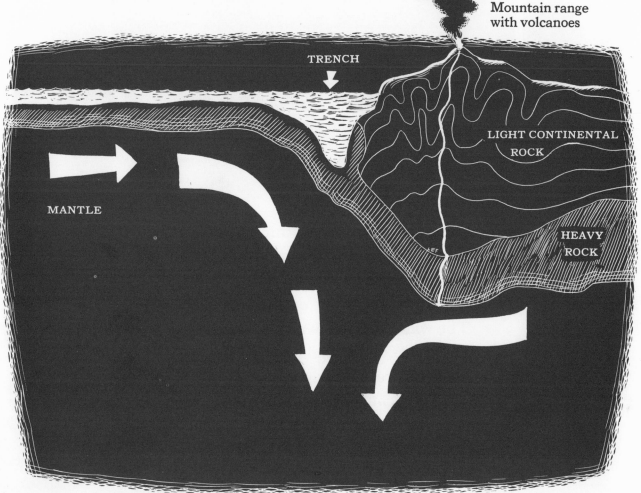

Mountain range
with volcanoes

TRENCH

LIGHT CONTINENTAL
ROCK

MANTLE

HEAVY
ROCK

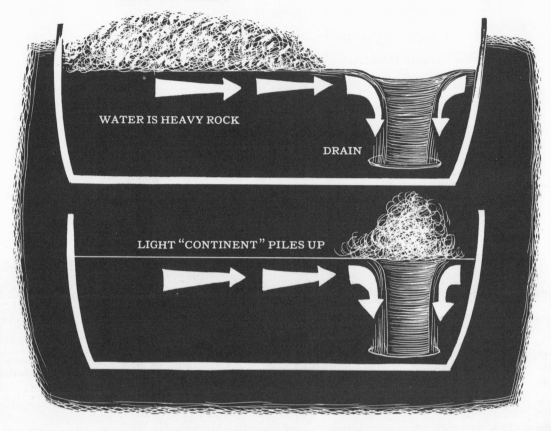

SUDS "CONTINENT"

WATER IS HEAVY ROCK

DRAIN

LIGHT "CONTINENT" PILES UP

What happens is something like
sudsy water going down a drain. Think of
a blob of suds as a continent, and the
flowing water as the ocean-floor rock.
The water flows down the drain easily.
But the suds only pile up
over the drain whirlpool.
This is because they are lighter
than the water beneath them.

The Rocky Mountains in North America
and the tall Andes in South America seem to
have formed because of
sinking movements in the crust.
"Ring of fire" islands such as those
off Alaska and Asia also seem
to have been made this way.

The Andes

The continents are still drifting
very slowly apart. Millions of years
from now, a map of our planet will
look different. Some convection currents
in the mantle may have stopped flowing
by then. And perhaps new ones
will start. This movement of the solid earth
will continue as long as there is
hot, liquid rock beneath us.

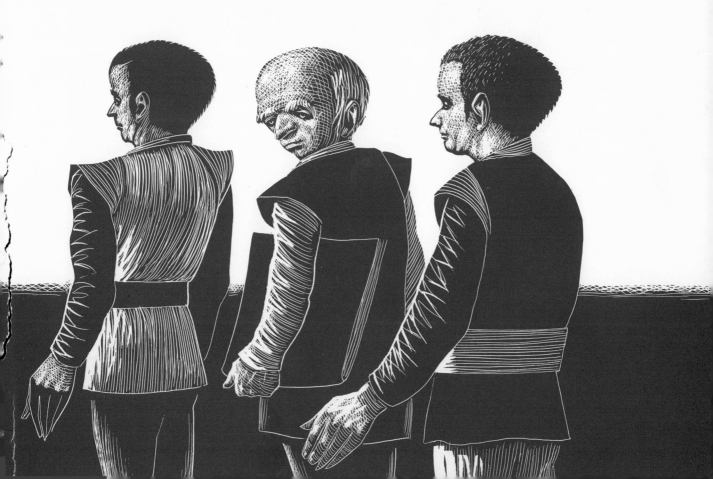